Lengthy Momentary Lapses on Purpose

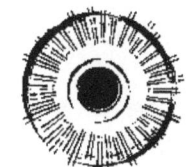

j.e.dante

Lengthy Momentary Lapses on Purpose
A Poetry Collection

Copyright © 2025 by j.e.dante

All rights reserved.
This book is protected by copyright. No part of this publication may be reproduced, distributed, or transmitted in any form or by any means, including photocopying, recording, or other electronic or mechanical methods, except in the case of brief quotations embodied in critical reviews and certain other noncommercial uses permitted by copyright law.

First Edition.
Published by: Dante Literary Press
ISBN-13: 979-8-9937795-0-8

Cover Design by: j.e.dante
Interior Design by: j.e.dante

For permission requests, write to the author at: danteliterarypress@gmail.com

[Allison]
for sending me down path I was meant to follow

[Harper and Declan]
for your big hugs and infectious laughter

[Mom and Dad]
for your grace in the face of great angst

I 13

- [Mud] 1
- [Brain Stew] 2
- [Blessed Sling] 3
- [Tarmac Tourniquet] 4
- [Gung-ho] 5
- [Cartography] 6
- [Chameleon on a Stick] 7
- [Addictive Personality Distorter] 8
- [Their Playing My Song] 9
- [Varicose Strains] 10
- [Everybody's Got One] 11
- [Premeditated Subjugation by Regurgitation] 12
- [Tomb Raider] 13
- [Medical Malpractice] 14

II 17

- [Crystalline] 19
- [Jury's Intuition] 20
- [Grey] 21
- [Constructive Criticism] 22
- [The Bulge] 23
- [Vindictive Coverts] 24
- [Seller's Market] 25
- [The Vilified Are Tried] 26
- [Tickled Pink] 27
- [Set the Table] 28
- [Hag] 29

[Mamacita] 30

[Accomplices be Damned] 31

[Chick Flicked Me] 32

[Devine Feminine] 33

[Where Do We Go When We Sleep] 34

[Satellite] 35

[Devaluations and Devolutions] 36

[Pepto Abysmal] 37

[Toasted] 38

[Bottomless Pit] 39

[Poker Face] 40

[Birthright] 41

[Holy War] 42

[Have Mercy] 43

[Won the Battle\\Lost the War] 44

[Speakeasy] 45

[Dumb Luck] 46

[Carousel Coliseums] 47

[Prickly Pear] 48

[Applesauce] 49

III 51

[TGIF] 53

[Negligence] 54

[Kites] 55

[Abstract Art] 56

[Green Behind the Ears] 57

[Never Alone] 58

[Hurrah] 59

[Ejaculate Misconception] 60

[Turtles Are Dinosaurs] 61

[Dime bag Overture] 62

[Unhinged] 63

[October] 64

[Pretty] 65

[Nine to Five] 66

[Tents] 67

[Farewell] 68

[Credence] 69

[Little Boy] 70

[Call Out King] 71

[Psychosis] 72

[Smartass] 73

[Mode to Unmask Us] 74

[Pillow Talk] 75

[Seasonal] 76

[Punch Out] 77

[Triple A] 78

IV 81

[Headstone] 83

[Likely Story] 84

[Sleeping Spell] 85

[Polarizing Adhesive] 86

[Sardine] 87

[Cabin Fever] 88

[She's a Charmer] 89

[Collateral Damage] 90

[Equal Signs and Arrows] 91

[USBS] 92

[Little Black Dress] 93

[The Showmen] 94

[Lengthy Momentary Lapses on Purpose] 95

[Messianic Hypothesis] 96

[Drizzle] 97

[Bloodsucker] 98

[Feet to the Ground] 99

[Milk Carton Evangelists] 100

[Traffic Cones] 101

[Half Cup] 102

[Severance] 103

[At What Cost] 104

[Serendipity] 105

[So Deep] 106

[American Fecal] 107

V 109

[Pragmatic Fanatic] 111

[Asylum] 112

[Harvest] 113

[Tanning Red] 114

[Watching Paint Dry] 115

[Exhausted Fumes] 116

[A Warning] 117

[Ghoulish] 118

[Island] 119

[Faded] 120

[Twelve Phases] 121

[Nineteen Ninety -Nine] 122

[Things Mothers Shouldn't See] 123

[Ashtrays] 124

[Folly] 125

[Proliferation's Discretion] 126

[Millisecond of Hell] 127

[Bolstering Your Breeches to Bursting] 128

[The Simple Things] 129

[String Theory] 130

[Here We Go Again] 131

[Poor Sport] 132

[First World Problems] 133

[Mannequin] 134

[Ellipsis] 135

[Black hole] 136

[Thoughts of You] 137

[Authors Note]

Welcome to *Lengthy Momentary Lapses on Purpose.*

    This collection is, in many ways, an echo chamber of the everyday internal monologue—the incessant "milling it over indefinitely," the silent arguments with oneself, and the often-unspoken observations of a world perpetually performing. These poems are born from the quiet anxieties, the sudden jolts of clarity, and the pervasive sense that, perhaps, we're all just figuring things out, or trying very hard not to.
    Within these pages, you'll find reflections on the intricate, sometimes maddening, landscapes of the mind, a wry commentary on the curious spectacle of humanity, and the relentless pull of existential questions that demand attention, even when we'd rather they didn't. There are moments of frustration, moments of unexpected connection, and moments where the only sensible response is a cynical laugh.
    Thank you for choosing to spend some of your own momentary lapses with this work. I hope you find a resonance, a challenge, or at the very least, a moment of quiet recognition.

I

*I write poetry
because I lack
The attention span
To be novel*

Lengthy Momentary Lapses on Purpose

[Mud]

My eyelids grow heavy,
weighted with hours spent,
the borrowed time bartered
to halt wayward descent.
My crutch that leads to bursting;
when I lack it,
there is such thirst.
Splitting my head right between the eyes:
A third opened giving words their birth.
Anxiety reverberates as I contact divinity.
Words whip with thick arithmetic.
Heart racing to discharge the buzzing
that so aggravates my psyche.
Exchanging the gas that keeps the car running
for the fuel that sends it into orbit,
wholly enveloped in the torrent.
The words flowing so fast and often
that the paper is hard-pressed to absorb it.
The shakes— My worthy associates.

j.e.dante

[Brain Stew]

Midnight murdered my mind,
muttered misuses.
My mental declined,
meddling morgue murmurs,
mirroring its crime.
Beneath the savored watch
of fermented incline,
cleverly sat sipping
the reddest of wine.

Lengthy Momentary Lapses on Purpose

[Blessed Sling]

Skipping rocks and kicking stones,
tempered scars and busted toes;
friendly walks with heavy woes,
pinnacle thoughts voice mighty foes.

j.e.dante

[Tarmac Tourniquet]

I'm an idiot who can shape words,
on occasion pull slick rhymes,
at times to appear well learned,
when in actuality,
I write to feel the sweet burn
of attention, gripping statically.
"Please don't let me go,
please don't let me go, please don't let me go."
Click.
Here we go again.
I drag myself through the gutter
to tear off another piece,
and then fend off the nervous energy
I've come to associate and comprehend
as my means to an applauded end,
just to shed my skin
and pick up wherever I began.
Doubtful that I'll ever tap that clarity
of thought again.
Vanity is a sin I pretend is my friend,
who takes me at face value,
akin to a thin grin.
Fin.

Lengthy Momentary Lapses on Purpose

[Gung-ho]

I delegate tasks to my many selves,
yearning for,
but lacking, linear split.
Sand slips upon politely dusted shelves,
meter counting on my wire to trip.
Tentative I traverse my biases,
them so keen to forgo diversity.
A perish of virus and recesses,
founded on self-served negativity.
Flipping the terminal switch,
I change the tune,
no longer investing inventory.
Capacity for tenacity doomed,
verse exploding into purgatory.

j.e.dante

[Cartography]

I'll siphon the prose consuming the gas,
welcome tones oblivious and deprived,
raised by fleeting intrigue.
Interests roar past,
inspiration revealed: fractions derived.
Melodramatic, I pass on context,
harping upon the timeless residue;
decidedly bloated petty nonsense,
rhetoric mindlessly emotes, lacks clue.
Deviously composed,
shrewdly quartered,
reclusive nature silent in visage;
be not thwarted by something so forward,
focused eyes leave conception diminished.
In jest, I suggest an end to finesse;
in profess, she expressed her lack of dress.

Lengthy Momentary Lapses on Purpose

[Chameleon on a Stick]

I'm hanging on the coattails
of someone else's success,
lazily stringing the words along
and claiming they're my best.
I'm white-knuckling,
crushed beneath the stress.
Hands communing
with the dark rings
that surround my broken neck,
casually passing judgement
to satisfy the flesh.

j.e.dante

[Addictive Personality Distorter]

With a preceding reputation that puffs my cheeks to bursting, zip-zap-zipping across the room— my little balloon, brimming with embellishments, shrieking to the tune of euphoric dissonance, complete with a vehement inclination to thrive on the echoes of my past accomplishments.
My death by a thousand cuts: the many lies I tell myself to remain relevant.
It'd be a shame if my sham fell by the wayside, my reverent disciples dispersed amongst more readily available nuances— just old news in the grand scheme of things, begotten and forgotten, like a curtain call for a mundane fiend.

[Their Playing My Song]

Maestro, strike me my tune!
You know that radical deluge— the one that plucks at my heartstrings, shaking me with energy beams, brandishing banshee screams, when all might be serene, rhythm continually coming clean.
You know I don't do well with silences; silence doesn't do so good with me.
Beat that drum, yack that trap, toot your horn! Let my wildest imagination flee unseen, for if I take another sashay toward quiet, there'll be no stopping that wind-tunnel dream.
For weeks, I'll lay a loveless lump, a dump only a shower stream can clean.

j.e.dante

[Varicose Strains]

Menial labors lack a made man's candor;
these sordid cracks mar bullied skin.
With crack of whip to squander whim,
marks wasted time as detested sin.
The eloquent whispers reside therein,
abstractly catalogued though purpose dim,
extrapolating something where nothing begins.

Lengthy Momentary Lapses on Purpose

[Everybody's Got One]

Hark, as I binge you feed,
ruthless assault without winner's fee,
aligning you with such dinner deeds
as curious follies and ventriloquizes.
Extraordinarily lavish,
so lush and green,
garnished spring colors humor hyperbole,
omniscient composure in soliloquy.
You are all friends
with what I want you to see.

j.e.dante

[Premeditated Subjugation by Regurgitation]

If I make a list of things to say
by repeating dialogue for fear of fray,
on the off chance that from the script I stray—
Penance I ask of you today
for roiling your time with hapless wordplay.

[Tomb Raider]

"Crowded crescendo" is my affliction;
it cleaves and clamors against my restive nature,
feigning coexistence with tradition,
mining pretended truths in nomenclature.
Corralling my thoughts
is like excavating ancient ruins,
in search of rocks.
I'm infatuated with the rich history,
but prescribe to the ripeness quartered in grit,
found as I sift silt and stone
in search of modern interpretations
that are more accommodating
to my shifty,
wishy-washy,
morally superior high ground.

j.e.dante

[Medical Malpractice]

Maybe we need bus stops for ambulances,
because you can't seem to stay on your feet.
"Punk rock hottie"— you've always got something to
say: P.h.D.s in political correctness,
taking stances on things just far enough away.
You'll stick it to the man from just out of sight,
because real-life problems?
They just might bite.

II

*Things that get easily confused
Idealistic and realistic
exquisite and bland*

[Crystalline]

You know when you close your eyes, and in that deep, dark, deprived corner of your existence, you can miraculously call forth minuscule blips that we've coined memories.
These sedentary life forms that perch just above the clouds of uncertainty, willing you to investigate with a strained gaze, implicating you in the treasonous act of squinting, scrunching those oyster shells so tight that they begin to split atoms of colors you can't possibly name.
Knowing I can only guess is the one true measure of deeper thought. Knowledge is simply a mire so foreign that rerouting courses to success ultimately sends you in the wrong direction.
There is sobriety in the realization that you don't know a damn thing about yourself, and it spells mortality for the benevolent ruler of wealth, whose gleaming crown intertwines itself with the comings and goings of times and minds.
Whom have had their moments played back to them by medium of glazed eyes, the same eyes that stooped them to early decline—for they dined and wined and wined and whined until such brilliant shine left them blind to everything except those northern light displays, played back in an array of pictures they will never define.
A blip, and then nothingness. A sign of the times. A final line telling an untimely resign.

j.e.dante

[Jury's Intuition]

The habitual misplacement of silence—
my casual excuse for its abuse.
A vast repertoire
for such a costly appliance:
a hangman strung from his noose.

Lengthy Momentary Lapses on Purpose

[Grey]

I draw a line within the earth's confine,
for practicality's purpose divined;
lavishly furnished on my person shines,
but my mind is a brine that proposes divide.

j.e.dante

[Constructive Criticism]

I've got this pressure in my chest—
a little beast that they call pride,
rearing its grotesque head,
roaring just to prove he can.
My insecurities dragging in tow,
on chains I try to hide in my back pocket.
At times the weight drops me to my knees,
small words rolling up my sleeves,
bloodying my knuckles as my brain pleads:
"Please just grow a thicker skin."

[The Bulge]

Intuition is but a litany of instincts, reverberated at a frequency unheard, jousting with low-flying subjects, teetering on the precipice of the absurd.
"What guile," they'll quest, as they astutely observe the man who would be king, bested by a little child.
Whom addressed his sire's would-be queen:
"Madam, I've inquired," said he who'd been touched.
"Gleaned what I could from a glorious hunch."
A curious flush rushed to her face, blushed red, a sweeping from seating to her feet instead.
"Of what do you accuse?"
"Quite a scandal I've deduced! What, my liege, protrudes from your illustrious muse? Can flower blossom façade as a gnarled root?"
Alas, sat man abashed and unamused by the most un-queenly, if ever there was a ruse.

j.e.dante

[Vindictive Coverts]

I find all art pretentious:
Every ink splotch, brush stroke, harmony, and note.
Original thought parades and blatant semblances in
tropes. I despise moments that I am meant to feel
moved, juxtaposed to profiles shaking with
trepidation.
I lament their choice in idols and heroes—
Father figures molded in saintly men,
with professional courtesies to boast.
A levitating man probably won't tell his secrets,
discouraging liabilities in their mounting prestige,
haloed delusions of their inner-born artists,
where satisfaction is quarantined:
A muck of pigheaded, disassociating narcissists.
What precarious lives we lead.

[Seller's Market]

The foundations cracked,
the walls are rotting through.
Every splintered board and holy war,
all the shingles that came unglued—
This house used to be home;
Now it's just a room without a view.
I'm digging through the rubble,
might need a bigger shovel,
as I'm left picking up
all the pieces of you.

j.e.dante

[The Vilified Are Tried]

He reaches out to give a hand— two for a fellow man, a mellow man, a level man. But bloated bellies burst. Drowned by residual light, treading water with tender might. What might could have bought me whilst for the surface you fight? But bloated bellies burst. Facilitated by a steady hand, revolver level, steady with shovel's glance— the lance that drives the words home. But bloated bellies burst.
I am but a tome, a bridge of hot air blown, king of the exchange, jester of fooleries writ. But bloated bellies burst.
I am the raptor fighting beyond hope, mother to swaddling babe's cognition, manifestation of an overachiever's disadvantage— my friendship measured on the backs of foes. I am the threshold. My bloated belly bursts.

[Tickled Pink]

A populace descended from the shallowest crusades;
their referendum suffers the sways of strays,
grinding milk-white bones to flour,
enlightenment soured hour by hour.
Valiant men stand upon podiums raised,
sifting through words while wise men graze.
Under pretense and conjecture,
an axiom is born,
benign hallucinations fracture realities torn.
Amongst the children,
not one can recall
how flooded waters grew
such stories so tall.

j.e.dante

[Set the Table]

Abused privilege,
or a microcosm of something much worse?
You claim divine intervention
with lesser renditions of faith,
hands folded to cover both of our eyes:
cowering, vulnerable, sightless.
Three times I counted
these things I cannot comprehend.
In this ignorant self-indulgence,
prodigal delusions are envisioned.
Alas, your allure is wasted on me.
Mentor me not with your false tongues.
You may be blind,
but I can see.

Lengthy Momentary Lapses on Purpose

[Hag]

So entered the era of the she beasts;
they slip through chasms not filled,
merely trodden.
A tangle of fur and blur of decrease,
identity stamped sodden and solemn.
Garnered pit plummets in esteemed fury,
policing that which outwits my control.
Untouchable confidant to worry,
outpacing the wills in contest of souls.
What sinking tooth bore me that night away,
dreamscape peppered with heartfelt swelter?
Too toiled in coils' utmost array,
I fear I've boiled the brew that bred her.

[Mamacita]

Seclusions spawning delusions; I can't stand to be alone. She reps public relations with nearly nothing on.
Little hellion with some skeletons in tow.
"Excuse me, mamacita, how low can you go?"
I lost the plot about the moment that she walked in— something about the way she holds herself is so inviting.
I'm frightened. Enlightened.
And that's about the moment that she sunk her teeth in. "Mama warned me about girls like you— betray your heart to a vixen. You'll be a martyr through and through."
But I never want this night to end.
Drag me into the mist, introduce me to my wits' end.
"Where do we go from here? Did we touch on something real? I never want this night to end. I'm bending over backwards just to see you again. Where do we go from here? Does it all just disappear?"
I was praying for a happy ending.
Now I can see that we were both pretending.

[Accomplices be Damned]

You're my murder mystery— a casual casualty to love.
Splashing here in puddles of blood,
disturbed you ask yourself,
"Just what have you done?"
Lift yellow tape, interrogate a smoking gun.
White lines surround everything you do.
Sirens abound, clashing red on blue.
If only you knew.
What would you do?
I think you would've too.

j.e.dante

[Chick Flicked Me]

What if self-imposed pageantry had not depicted my youth— that delicate tape spun for every moment reached with intention, segregated by the cues that subdued the picture-perfect scene?
Had I the intuition to reign in sunlight, to embrace that femininity beneath such a milky galaxy, would I have relinquished the rights to this production as it now tells?
Perspective in a backward glance cuts ties with perchance and replaces the script with her entrance into my scene: a slow-motion descent, splashing white light from Christmas strings, earmarking my mouth agape and my person held hostage by a crescent and a bun that speaks of an afterthought.
As my muddy shoes stained her mother's carpet, my heart groaned, assuming mistakes in moving day's downturned delivery— an angel entered our midst.
I would be remiss if I told a differentiated twist. Hollywood will never tell it better than this. I've loved her every moment since.

Lengthy Momentary Lapses on Purpose

[Devine Feminine]

Machines, fuel and fire are
the nature of a strong-willed man.
He beds and breaks bread with desire,
agonizing over where he must stand.
He balances strength and spitfire,
but inherently craves
the governance of a matron.

j.e.dante

[Where Do We Go When We Sleep]

The time to settle the score came and went;
I meandered corridors gone endless,
eager to be swept beyond callousness.
My bed portals to the hour-less pent.
Salivating pistons push me further;
visitation becomes mandatory.
Every darkened sky exudes precursor,
sureness lacks surrounding category.
I won't promise equality tonight;
destinations aren't predetermined,
likened to daydreams.
Sight gleaned beyond sight,
reality never really certain.
Wrenched from the pattern,
tearing a path between stars.
Backwards I fell forward:
cold sweats in strange cars.

Lengthy Momentary Lapses on Purpose

[Satellite]

Catching flame, I plummet;
just couldn't deny the gravity.
Disengaged from my surroundings,
entertaining the fragility.
A piece of paper, liable to tear
at the slightest flare,
like that thinly sliced tree I'm formed.
Deceased, but born;
born of those reclaimed materials,
soaked, pressed, and hung out to dry up.
As forbearers lending forget-me-nots,
baring my legacy in eulogy.
Penned words I hope to last long past me,
recycling ideas until they outlast the sun.
Many pieces pass into consortium;
they were mine to give,
and yours to consume.
Destined to survive my impending doom.

j.e.dante

[Devaluations and Devolutions]

Devotion shares a razor edge with delusion,
unloading and corroding,
blasting holes in conviction,
dismembering any inkling of reservation.
Rhyme and reason become the rind of capability,
all the while doing a disservice to the
shred of decent intellect I possess.
Fending the whirling stick with my own,
vandalizing the simple perfection that I host—
A crass derivative I've grown to loathe.

Lengthy Momentary Lapses on Purpose

[Pepto Abysmal]

If memory soon passes itself to the everlasting void,
sense of recall a luxury of the past.
Younger tongues unleashed at last,
may you wonder at the crass acts I've amassed—
the fire in my belly that passed as gas.

j.e.dante

[Toasted]

Define love without language;
don't pay me lip service on repeat.
Anyone can say, "I love you."
I want to know what it really means.
I want to cower from the blaze,
I want to be engulfed in timeless heat.
I don't want the mere words;
I want the words to make my heartbeat.

Lengthy Momentary Lapses on Purpose

[Bottomless Pit]

I long for the easy life,
to strike it rich and cleanse my palate
of the mundane necessities,
living out the rest of my days
wishing for nothing.
Except that the slow degradation
of my human experience
would leave me haunted and hollow enough
to appreciate having a reason to exist.

j.e.dante

[Poker Face]

The atrocity of meritocracy
is that it can never truly exist
when geezers, preachers, and diplomats
all clench their meaty myths.
After all,
there's no need for action
when you're filthy fucking rich.

[Birthright]

Life's a crap shoot:
You trip, stumble, and fall into self-awareness,
become cognizant of your egregious mistake,
and spend the next eighty years
second-guessing how you'll be remembered—
Only for your crowning achievements
to be incontinence and forgetting how to eat.

j.e.dante

[Holy War]

Arise and conquer,
for life is a fleeting illusion.
Death reaps what is sown;
cataclysm forever an eventuality.

[Have Mercy]

No, I don't subscribe
to your half-baked,
substance-less,
self-help bullshittery.
Let me rot.

j.e.dante

[Won the Battle\\Lost the War]

The regret consumes me as you fade into the night.
Taste the sickness that corrupted my lips— my faucet
of a mouth, hemorrhaging words ripped straight from
hastily penned manifestos fleeing the scene of a crime,
distributing first drafts as tenth editions.
Munitions closing the distance between pretty little
ears and puppy dog eyes, squandering your beauty as
liquid crystals well up the ductwork.
Our moment past at last, snuffed with no recourse. I'll
suffer you the discourse: A moment shy and a minute
too late.
I'll swear that I love you, and that it never was a lie.
But great expectations— they are creeping; they've
eaten me alive.

[Speakeasy]

I suffer a compulsion to be impulsive;
my weakness's propulsion.
Asphyxiation through aspiration,
attrition my damnation.

j.e.dante

[Dumb Luck]

I must have won some cosmic lottery the day our lives collided. The statistical probability we'd find each other amongst a backdrop of eight billion bleeding hearts feels like some fortunate misunderstanding, like a flash in a pan that refused to quit, or a shot in the dark that miraculously smack-dabbed us dead center mass of the habitable zone.
Like some universal entity wanted justification for the precise nature of galactic spacing, and math just couldn't cut it— the stratosphere drawn up as a commission to give trees a chance to fill our lungs, to beat the hearts in our chests, to drive our precious meat suits together in life, in love, in matrimony, in childbearing, in old age, and even in death. I don't believe much in luck; it feels like a poor excuse for failure. But if it did exist on this plane, I think I've used all mine up.

Lengthy Momentary Lapses on Purpose

[Carousel Coliseums]

We're all just trying to get the last word
in an endless go-around
between masking disingenuousness
and simply not giving a shit.

j.e.dante

[Prickly Pear]

There's just enough ambition in me
to seethe when I see other people succeed,
and just enough guilt
to just give them their flowers.

[Applesauce]

I detested your restlessness— your flighty, fidgety fingers fumbling over frigid scaffolding, haphazardly slapped between tall, decrepit elevator pitches and streets that reek of piss. Your amber twitching harbingers, all keyed up in anticipatory lunacy, strung out on bed bugs, smog, and sewer rats, consistent with the size of smaller canine breeds. Homesick and sleepless without the rising tension of checkered horns billowing in the streets, surrounded by cracking concrete that apparently never sleeps.

III

I loved with abandon
She took her time
Now we're both alone

[TGIF]

"Could you cut me a mixtape? I want to disassociate; fast-forward to the end of the week." But every time Friday rolls around my way, it kind of loses all its mystique.
I spend four whole days hoping, and on the fifth start coping as the final two start to creep. And just like that, a week turns into four; another dozen, and the Reaper's out here begging for more.
A premature countdown to another perfect letdown. There's no space in time I can find to escape every wishful thought of you. So, forgive me, if I'm skewed blue; I'm seeing ghosts since you left some screws loose. I would kill for a better excuse, but the tick-tock of the clock sucks the life out of living.
I've got a thousand-kilometer stare to pair with a million-dollar smile. If you didn't notice, I'm the hostess with the most-est: a nihilistic sense of denial. "Thank God it's Friday!" Too bad my calendar won't set me free. I'll sacrifice sleep for leisure, pack my whole life between ten and three. I'll ask: "Why the fuck am I always tired? When the hell am I going to retire?" The finish line's too far away to see. So, for now, I'll procrastinate, stay up way too late, and hope the red eyes don't catch up with me.

j.e.dante

[Negligence]

Licking lips glisten bile,
billow blazes forth conceived.
Rancid taste of reconcile,
bringing rattles to my knees.
Ghastly premonitions lost,
no adoration poured.
My heavy-handed drought so tossed,
personage now adorned.
Naught sense left spared to delve,
nor perching song choir.
Heavenly mirage beheld,
lurching from the fire.
A tear I urge for you,
my dear, barren beyond reason breaks.
To crack these wasteland slits so dry,
lend mercy at the gates.

[Kites]

She sniffed, crimson drip staining her linen,
horoscope double dipping from lined paper,
tracing a chaliced quip in a rounded capsule,
pistol-whipping her into unsettling sleep.
Up, up, and away until decency forsook her,
double-jointed free fall stretching her thin,
demanding a flight of stairs ascended,
a knob turned, and a long breath in.
Upon the high-rise she's met
with the yellow eyes of nine lives: arched back, gaping
jowls, flicking tail seeming to surmise.
Guttural vibrations rousing her from sleep,
bladed pupils compelling such prophetic notions as:
"Am I truly in love, or in love with the idea?" and
"Are all the stars in the universe truly ours to count?"
She shivers, naked toes hugging
brick and mortar precipice,
wind billowing golden locks
for the locksmiths to venerate.
She jumps for joy and does not envy the cat.

j.e.dante

[Abstract Art]

The shadows, they creep up the wall as I sleep, leading me to doubt I ever slept at all. The wisps in my dreams lead me to believe that there was hope in not believing at all.
Her melody haunts me as I lay my head to rest, bitter accomplice to my lack of confidence. If there was a lick of honesty that passed those lips, I can't recall. The breeze never brought me that news.
When you say that you're done to the barrel of a gun, one-way ticket stamped to outer space, will you even hear a bang or taste the salty spray of the loved ones you left behind as you float away?
Life doesn't always make sense at the time, full of imperfections that do not rhyme. Some days just seem like the sun won't shine, and every drop of melancholy steals your mind and robs you blind.
Onto her knees she pleads:
"Oh god, the novelty is wasted on me!"
With a click, her problems splash across the wall.

[Green Behind the Ears]

By the skin of my teeth
and the sweat that pours from my brow,
I've carved an intricate reputation,
notch by notch I've carefully fashioned these scars;
I sang the words you wanted to hear,
superficial and obscure.
They were just enough for a little while,
until decency walked out that door.
Let's settle the score.
As subtle flame flickers,
no damned fluorescent to bite,
and I'll wager a little more than crinkled paper—
cast my lots into the night.
"Does it hurt when you bleed?
I'll show you what it means to be unclean.
Didn't ask for sympathies,
beg for your mercy.
Don't tally me amongst the sinners that you've freed.
Only God can save filthy old me."
I spend most of my nights a ragging,
never felt the calm before the storm.
I was bred a beast of burden,
only I was cursed with the desire for more.
"Oh, the grass isn't greener on the other side," they
say— "be pragmatic, optimistic, ethical until you grey."
But if I turn another cheek, take heat again today,
I promise it won't be your feet
that carry you out of this place.

j.e.dante

[Never Alone]

I am acutely aware of my clandestine hosts;
I've made friends with those decomposed.
Though we are not defined by the coffins hidden so
carefully beneath the floorboards,
not swayed by the ghosts of an echoey past,
I fear I'll never lack company again.

Lengthy Momentary Lapses on Purpose

[Hurrah]

When sweet dispositions muster broke,
twisted and tangled by the passing of days,
programming disrupted by the parting of ways.
Rolling hills ventured as far as sight permitted,
kept ants marched with file befit:
a great spectacle to behold,
my captive audience of wit.
Observers well-meaning,
soldiers I commit.

j.e.dante

[Ejaculate Misconception]

I commissioned a crook who stole all my things,
sold me quick pleasures devoid of all strings.
Pitched me the sky, didn't mention the wings.
Rented out my time to whomever he pleased—
the subjugating pull of natural tendencies,
melting the lewd goop into lucid dreams,
the merging of webbing and idolatries.
That man stole from me my flesh
and sold me fleshy screens.
The fine print, an edging of responsibility,
may be addicting, the afflicted text reads:
"Once you've peeked, you may never leave."

[Turtles Are Dinosaurs]

There was a caustic sensibility in the way
she gouged her lower lip,
the type of symbolism that poets overlook
in the pursuit of symmetry.
Overbite marketed salaciously,
whetting one's appetite.
Her compelling, matured tractor beams—
a vice grip.
Titillating heart purring where it most pleases,
in the same vein as the abstract circuitry
that necessitates pissing on trees.

j.e.dante

[Dime bag Overture]

Like schoolyard romantics believe in destiny,
we get all tangled up in between the sheets.
Maybe we just suffer from chronic naivety;
the gravity of our trajectory is enough to suspend belief.
The chill disassociates the flame from its heat;
passion makes way for crimes of passionate deceit.
Maybe I'm just a sucker for the way things used to be,
I can't discern the differences
between good health and depravity.
You can't stand it when I stand tall on my own two feet. Heaven forbid I clash with your fragile masculinity.
You're jealous when I go out; we fight when I stay in.
I'm really starting to question
what the hell we're even doing.
Executioner, judge, and jury—
the way you're eyeing me is making me worry.
So let's sniff another bag,
take another drag, let's cast ourselves into oblivion.
Let's down another beer, afraid to be sincere,
let's objectify our delusions.
You've got me on the ropes; you've cashed in all my hope for late nights and moral quandaries.
I feel I sold my soul, digging deep, dark holes,
to manifest synchronicity.
But we can't stand to be lonely.
Maybe we both need some time, because lately, baby, convenience has left us blind.
We just don't add up. We both feel fed up.
Let's call it while we still have the time.
It will hurt now, but it'd be so much worse down the line.

[Unhinged]

Hindsight is no friend to comfort;
I wish the words hadn't parted my lips.
The turning of a new leaf
inviting my mind to wander,
its fallen companions lonely
upon the autumn breeze.
Their pallet a colorful wash
against the dull blue sky of me.
Routine dulls the edges
and tears me at my seams;
my solid vision fractured and trampled,
a million shards beneath my feet.
For six long nights I sat by my lonely,
inner monologue composing
symphonies of self-doubt and denial,
preaching words that I'll seldom repeat.
The current dragging me into the deep.
It's at this point I realize I'm asleep:
unfathomable depths
nothing more than mere puddles
ankles deep.
Asleep at the wheel,
I'm weaving between lines
that aren't even real,
putting my head down,
hoping that people will just steer clear.
This is my fear:
to climb these mighty mountains,
to sit atop their snow-dusted peaks,
just to ignore the view.
Because whenever I look
upon this landscape of me,
all I see is you.

j.e.dante

[October]

Visions in the dark—
such a funny thing, really,
that we can touch
without ever truly feeling.
Vibrant emotions
pushed beneath the surface;
odds and ends,
bits and pieces,
with no realized purpose.
But every dream,
no matter how fleeting,
keeps troubled men sane
and lovers' hearts beating.

Lengthy Momentary Lapses on Purpose

[Pretty]

Screw your politics;
I don't care about your views.
Embrace the sunless waste
of introspective hullabaloo.
If you could shake the hate
you regurgitate from tiny screens,
maybe you'd have
a different definition of what it all means.
But you're too pretty.
So damn pretty. Pretty fucking sad.
You've always got the correct words to say,
arguments to make the facts
all go so stinking far away.
But can you close your eyes
and hold your spine straight?
Take me as I am
and quit making an interstate of your arm's length.
But you're too pretty.
So damn pretty. Pretty fucking sad.
Tell me, honey, how your traps hold up your head.
Yeah, the neck is pretty great,
but your noggin's full up with lead.
You say you want to recap,
you want to redo,
but every time I spell it out,
you kind of make it all about you.
But you're too pretty.
So damn pretty. Pretty fucking sad.
You're f-u-c-k-i-n-g sad. You've got a pretty face,
but a waste of space past that.
I've got to wave Sayonara; I've got to bid thee adieu
soon, because when you shimmy out your skimpies,
the air's going to leave the room.

j.e.dante

[Nine to Five]

What if we never outgrew Velcro,
stumbling between "to" and "from,"
tangled in tangible laces that
were never taught to tie themselves,
stowed inside sneakers blushingly unanchored,
stumbling over a quarrelsome and neglected tutelage?
Quite a quandary the beeps of this checkout line
produce: size eleven and a half heartbreakers stowed,
pinned deep between arm and torso.
The attendant and I exchange ocular sympathies,
rationalizing silently our laceless shoes.
As if our *faux pas* sense of mutuality established a
foundation from which to catacomb every late night
and work trip someone close ever took,
gratefully bitter towards the security that obscured
how more presence in our lives might look.

[Tents]

I went on a burnt-out renaissance of a bender,
omnipresent hysterias and their tongue-in-cheek.
Per-chanced a glance at a summer swim hole
sweetheart, emerging from the depths of sun-soaked
pipe dreams, ripples embracing crease.
Formative fodder and photographic fortune flit
between exuberant coral
and the epidermis that flaunts it,
willing perplexing waves to crash
upon the backs of unsuspecting victims,
relinquishing them from their salacious fabrics
so that Atlanteans might find intrigue
in recycling them as quilts,
and that I might have a view.
But alas, this isn't a wave pool,
and she isn't interested.

[Farewell]

The long-awaited voyage
to a place unknown,
I will sail alone.
As the anchor lifts,
I say my farewells;
shed no tears for me,
my place is on the open sea.
Like the tides, I can never stay;
the current pulls me out.
My guide, my peace, my rest—
show me the way, oh sirens' song,
show me the place that I belong.
Through the storm, they call to me;
light the way when I am lost,
my beacon to the great beyond.
Amid thunder's crash and lightning's glare,
ever will you guide my sail.
A lost soul I am not.
Fate is my vessel, my guide is the sea.
Forever may I wander, forever may I be
at peace, alone at sea.

[Credence]

When sub-par apparitions project lucidly,
malignant stew seduces surfeit misery.
Preordain your tragedy;
denounce liberty,
degrade your autonomy,
never be received.

j.e.dante

[Little Boy]

I've got sticky fingers and a big bad bomb,
a Fat Man stuffed with uranium.
Oppenheimer, you know you've got my heart.
Won't you shred my atoms,
tear me all apart?
You can't course correct
this payload at thirty thousand feet.
I've weaponized this hard head of mine;
won't compromise defeat.
Matter soon won't matter
in the face of all this heat.
Behold my meteor of conceit;
watch as my devils feast.
The cortex is a vortex
of hot-blooded ambition,
full of big rocks in loincloths,
finger-painted cave renditions.
Ignite the electronics,
crack the tectonics.
Insight: supersonic fission.
This is, in fact, the last earthly transmission.
I've got a handful of the sun;
the son's got a death grip on me.
God's not amused by my egocentricity.

[Call Out King]

On weekdays, before your cranium rolls sideways,
and you find yourself free
from fluffy feathered highways,
the bell tolls, and you start to depress,
because you don't want to find yourself slipping
the slope between jobless, hopeless, and homeless.
You do your best to assess
every trouble, malady, and stress,
attest to why it is you're not feeling your very best,
distressed over the slightest inconvenience and mess.
Deduce the smallest excuse and abuse it;
ruminate every sickly detail, recuse it.
So, when boss man tries to exhume it,
he'd be hard-pressed not to excuse it.

j.e.dante

[Psychosis]

Instigate, retaliate, then play the victim.
Drive home crying at midnight,
making a crisis out of slices of life,
when it's less about being right
and more about making light
of how everyone else is so wrong.
Chilling atop a soapbox,
filthy as all hell,
preaching unholy verses
full of pervasive, persuasive, perverse, and perverted,
pious, and subverted one-liners—
devoid of gravitas, full of ego, undisputed.
The champion of delusion is crowned.

Lengthy Momentary Lapses on Purpose

[Smartass]

Someday something nasty's
going to sneak up and bite me.
And for all the hours
I've spent fantasizing
that very moment,
all I'll have to show
is my wit.

j.e.dante

[Mode to Unmask Us]

I was born guilt-ridden;
They named her Grace.
She wielded crests and troughs
like a fiery saber.
I ran like hell,
cursing her name,
until utter black reigned.
She took my hand,
I, ashamed.
Flee.
I could never make her.

[Pillow Talk]

I could hear you weep,
feel you creak
as you drenched the sheets.
And maybe I should just
go back to bed,
pull up the covers
before I fill up my head
with the wrong ideas.
But let's be real:
that ship has sailed
seven seas and back,
and still hasn't satisfied
your lust to wander.
And now I'm left to ponder
if I'm just a means to an end,
and she's just biding her time
for a quick getaway.

j.e.dante

[Seasonal]

Wildflowers—
they will come and go.
They don't follow rules
that tell them where to grow.
And I will be so grateful
that I got to know,
so lucky that I got to bask
in your glow.

Lengthy Momentary Lapses on Purpose

[Punch Out]

Should the good Lord
take me away from you,
know that you will never,
ever be alone.
I will be upstairs
looking after you.
Just know:
You will always have
in me a home.

j.e.dante

[Triple A]

I've spent my whole life hoping
that all my hard work would pan out.
The rage that fueled my twenties
would quell all the self-hate and deep doubt.
But nothing seems forthcoming;
dedication doesn't equate to shit.
I was put onto this planet
to auto-draft until my ghost gives.
Now I don't mean to be mopey,
or for my heartache to seep out.
It's getting harder to wear a brave face,
trying to suck it up when I'm burnt out.
So please don't send me your letters,
no fancy invitations.
I will cordially decline them,
mark them all zero plus none.

IV

*come wilt with me
let our blistering heat
feed us to the ground*

[Headstone]

I'm feeling kind of manic,
just a hopeless romantic.
Welcome to the cynic clinic,
where it's been a pleasure
trying to be your pain.
Wax and wane,
cause some strain,
casting shadows,
throwing shade.
Impulse is to misbehave;
flowers on my grave.

j.e.dante

[Likely Story]

Kindling within the shrine of soul,
I hold the keys to a world all my own,
because below there is only room to grow.
Roots to branches, time will show
how the seeds that were planted
became something whole.

[Sleeping Spell]

I'm your weathered street-sweeper,
sweeping while you sleep, salvaging warped
observations, crumpled newspapers in heaps.
Oh, Tasty treats, tasty treats.
I'm your prescribed source of convection, lady;
word vomit's my true source of introspection lately.
As we ascend to perfection,
can't help but to consent to the infection, baby.
Stating my complexion made me.
"God save me! I'm so damn lazy! Am I crazy?
God, please save me!"
Pour it out to the paper; make friends with lead.
When I sink to the depths, you reach out from the
edge. "Am I dead?" She said, "It's all in my head."
Tasty treats, tasty treats. Your heart beats for me,
chasing dreams, mending seams. Tolls aren't ever
free,
my baby. Queenly lady.
Intertwined, drain my mind, she's enshrined.
My storm quelled to solace—
unrefined, endless pine—I need time.
I'm a work in progress.
Gently drift to sleep, rest your weary eyes,
weave dreams as I sweep. I'll be there when you rise.

j.e.dante

[Polarizing Adhesive]

These are the public enemy's numbering one,
subverts who're wallowed, willing, and waiting,
pondering morons frivolously throwing bones,
their insolence begetting castrating.
I'm not particularly interested in people
scrubbing the floor with my face,
but for the meanwhile, content to just let it slide.
To pacify their groping stances, I won't vilify the pace.
Begrudged children looking with solvent eyes
toward charismatic gentlemen guised:
Testaments of triumph, true and tried.

[Sardine]

The contrarians dismounted posture,
whines and raves against those they deem obtuse.
Foliage teems with long-winded talkers,
contradicting themselves in chorused spruce.
Prim and proper, they stride in leveled gate,
candidly depreciate the demand,
sweeping and cleansing the conflicted slate,
donning skeletons as works of their hands.
Reverend to the epitome of yesteryears,
shepherded procession so cordial,
exaggerating themselves so sincere,
in the process, becoming quite normal.
By fate extortion, dropped you from graces,
not one distinguished in sea of faces.

j.e.dante

[Cabin Fever]

As skyscrapers sway above urban heights,
do they bask in the ever-present glow?
Have they need for silence's still respite?
Ever once glowered at rural meadow?
Devised schemes exchanging cement for dirt?
Befriended birds roosted in transit?
Cursed the heavens for making them inert,
but giving them the height to be romantic?

[She's a Charmer]

Her eyes— a monument to disregard,
hiding within a faulted cause.
Triumph measured only in tears;
she is oblivious to it all.
Kind words, an afterthought
to what's meant,
just another soul rendered meaningless.
Her eyes— veiled, they speak volumes.
Beckon you in.
Yet romance is dead and gone,
like dust to the wind.
She will overlook,
kindles the flame,
just to watch it burn you alive.
Standing in the ashes,
she fulfills her need.

j.e.dante

[Collateral Damage]

In this painted landscape of you,
we are all just falling stars,
crashing and burning into your atmosphere.
How many times will we let ourselves be shot down
before we realize there's a life outside those eyes,
oh, ever so inviting?
I'm a lost cause; she's already closed the doors,
double-checked the locks on my heart.
When I close my eyes, I can feel her lips.
Forgetting her is out of the question.
She is my drug, and I need my fix,
my one and only, my last obsession.

[Equal Signs and Arrows]

And there she was,
my little supersonic squirmer,
shooting straight through the cobwebs and scars,
straight past the subjective podiums
and the custodians that keep them.
Is she my soothing savior?
The flames still reside,
but somehow easier to hide,
extinguished if desired.
I am not what I once was,
nor what I will soon become.
I am just here, plastered to this monitor,
looking at you with reinvigorated eyes—
my daughter.
What did I do to deserve such a lullaby?

j.e.dante

[USBS]

"Please return to sender," she doesn't live here
anymore. The wizard of compulsion repurposed a
butter knife, mischievous makeshift lawbreaker,
nicked, then picked through mail, justifying itself as
reward for resurrecting a trail of curled locks from a
drain.
Nauseating entertainment in bills to be paid,
connecting the dots like roads to be paved.
There are cracks in my cement
with weeds to be sprayed.

[Little Black Dress]

Disaster struck twice tonight;
this evening the toll was two.
Immaculate shag talks of rugged hue,
perspiration dewing filaments with delight.
Jazzily consternated by thrashing limbs,
intertwined in their chosen manner,
in the way that they so love to do.
Sensing imminent bashing of glassware
in cosmopolitans poured for two,
flinging acrid saturation,
mingled comet tails
gangling unceremoniously about the room.
Big Bang unfolding the cosmos—
simply the culmination of letting loose.

j.e.dante

[The Showmen]

Spinning in circles on little toes,
the world in motion as a smile grows.
The seed is the rhythm,
clapped in time to the beat,
exalted on high
through blur of feet.

[Lengthy Momentary Lapses on Purpose]

Fortune favors frequency,
but frequently
I favor milling it over indefinitely,
vicariously picturing the rise and fall
of my fortunate success,
concluding that fortune is not worth
the successive monotony.

j.e.dante

[Messianic Hypothesis]

Spring was the burgundy overcoat that draped itself
unobtrusively across my shoulders,
a webbed gleam through the trees
to compliment those light-padded forest critters,
scribbling along on errands long overdue,
or perhaps they were just trying to marginalize me,
an unwarranted guest in their homely neck.
Regardless, as the path swelled to its justification,
it seemed to me that the world
opened itself to interpretation.
If not for the first time, this time indeed,
nature cornered me within a backdrop of such
magnificence and grandeur
that I could scarce observe all that was seen.
It teemed with such tender essence in trickling
streams—
little fingers stretching so long
they forgot from where they'd come.
I find it all inconsequential to the scheme,
as sensory overload unveils itself,
my dilemma in this scene.
My perception is the limit,
making the whole a holy dream.
The black holes of oblivion lay
as satire's foolhardy regime.

[Drizzle]

The pavement glumly glistens;
greedy puddles lap at feet.
Stoic leaves take their mark;
rabid rapids mount concrete.
Beaded stained glass glistens,
those devilish guard of gloom.
Restless, cloudy, weighted traps,
sentencing life served within my room.

j.e.dante

[Bloodsucker]

It's just a smile, a sarcastic upturn of the lip.
This punchline lost its sharpness on the tip of my
tongue. I've been bit. I've been bit.
Spewing hot venom, I'll lap up every word.
A forked road, a forked tongue.
This is my liberation;
I'm cross-eyed in contemplation.
If left is right, and right is what's left,
nothing I say will ever be blessed.
I'll take to the ground, writhe with the snakes.
Take a bite from an apple— that's all it takes.

Lengthy Momentary Lapses on Purpose

[Feet to the Ground]

To what end?
We walk down this empty street
to another crossroads, to another week.
Countless are the hours spent—
well spent or not—
they are all gone now.
Somewhere.
Somewhere else.
Anywhere else.
We walk on...
To what end?

j.e.dante

[Milk Carton Evangelists]

Everyone's so enraptured with rapture,
hog-tied by falling skies
and biblical catastrophes,
tripping over secular harpings.
Harbingers of good news and tough luck,
rolling out the five Ws like merchants of death.
The sometimes Hs
conveniently swept alongside the riff-raff
beneath expensive Persian rugs,
constructing monumental escalators,
taking one small step over man,
hurdling mankind's plight with flight.
Heat-seeking sniffers honed to the heavens,
salivating over salvation
while skipping every step.

Lengthy Momentary Lapses on Purpose

[Traffic Cones]

I had an epiphany the other day
of all the things I didn't say:
How all the words in the world
couldn't have stopped you from leaving,
how I didn't even try to stand in your way.

j.e.dante

[Half Cup]

There's poison in the well
that I've been drinking
from for years,
full of all the hours spent
wishing you were here.

[Severance]

Sell me down the river, ship me out to sea.
When you say forever, tell me what you mean.
Because you've been kind of distant,
I've been lost in waking dreams.
When he talks, you're intent,
but you never listen to me. You're shady.
And we'll fly, fly until the sky stops.
Love won't die until our hearts stop.
My heart stopped when he stole you away,
and you lay unashamed.
Recite your vows for the congregation,
amuse yourselves beneath the sheets.
Appreciate these precious moments;
it makes no difference to me.
I pray he makes you happy.
Curse the moisture on your lips.
I've sent the hounds out hunting.
I settle my debts in pounds of flesh.
Then you'll cry, leak until the pulse stops.
Daisies rise, chest-bursting little sundrops.
Blood slops, headstone marking the place
where your misery lays.
Black veil masks her consternation.
Silence echoes around the room.
Trap doors give way to torment.
I fall, a man consumed.

j.e.dante

[At What Cost]

I lay awake, filling the space with you,
longing to chase your frame through the dark,
imagining your silhouette dancing about the room,
like trying to explain away an unfinished tattoo.

[Serendipity]

I had spent the morning dropping off the corpses of yet another wasted opportunity, when you descended a flight in a cascade of white, tangled in Christmas lights, sloppy bun all askew. I caught a view of a crescent moon tattoo, and she told me, "Boy, I'm going to marry you someday," and I can't tell you why, but that sounded "A" okay. And it's a mystery to me how you could pick this loser without a penny to my name. You said, "Fuck it, let's drive forever." And it's hard to explain, and I might risk sounding a little insane, but from the second I held you, I knew shit was going to change; the moment that I kissed you, my whole life got rearranged. Black cats and quarrels over coffee, never nearly enough cash, moving so damn fast. I gave you a key: "Share a roof with me." Shacked up after too few months on nothing but a hunch. Subtle aren't we? So, kiss me, mama, make my heart leap straight out my chest, lady. Dance all around me, won't you love me, baby? Put your hands all over me, because ever since we've been together, it's always serendipity.

j.e.dante

[So Deep]

All you aesthetic stoics are a bunch of measly,
measured masochists,
pigeonholing yourselves as knights
upon the roundest of tables,
conveniently perched
above the carnal passions
of peasants, princesses,
and their high towers.
Slyly morphing peculiar thoughts
into blatant self-obsession,
becoming the serpents you love to detest,
nesting in burrows brimming
with signaled virtue and bad breath.

[American Fecal]

If our worth is the summation of what we know,
then maybe lining embroidered pockets
with loose change reclaimed
from asphalt-covered interstates
could be some trendy new aesthetic
that takes the youth by storm.

V

the sedative didn't take
so here I'll lay
dreaming up words I will never say

[Pragmatic Fanatic]

I am enamored with the cyclical nature
of my own existence.
I've acclimated time after time,
squeezing myself into smaller and smaller,
sickly fractions, eliminating factions of my former self.
The proverbial boiling pot of self-actuation,
whose positive negativity persuades the mercury
into a ponderous upward trend.
I am eager to discover an irrefutable, indisputable
conclusion to this prolonged mess of autonomy,
evidence that tilts the trajectory an inch to the left
toward universal credibility.
What then will preside when it's made clear
we search for naught?
The answer truly is the lack of explanation.
What then will become of our compositions,
articulated of our own accord, with no formula to fit?
We are governed by that which will never know
understanding. Evidently, it is because it is.

j.e.dante

[Asylum]

I'm beaten, I'm tattered, I'm torn to shit.
I got a car full of baggage, and I'm drowning in debt.
I need a quick fix to make this all go away.
I need a quick fix. Doc, what do you say?
I want a back-alley lobotomy to set me free.
This is my destiny; do me this courtesy.
I want to cut all ties with my sanity.
I don't want no clarity. Life would be so easy—
a little pinch and a nosebleed.
It doesn't have to be complicated.
It doesn't have to be hard.
I don't want to be emasculated,
but my brain is charred.
Break me down into a hundred million pieces,
suffocate all my notions and thoughts.
I want my heart to be beating,
but with the lights all turned off.
I'm spinning my wheels
trying to get me ahead,
but every inch I get closer, I take two back instead.
So, I'll read some self-help, get some therapy,
but that shit is such a drag.
I just want a pinch and a nosebleed.

Lengthy Momentary Lapses on Purpose

[Harvest]

I'm sick of waiting for the click-clack
of train tracks to carry this heavy load—
it's cargo it never knows.
Met a stranger once,
running to catch up at a crossroads,
tail tucked between his pitiful, shaking legs,
while the gallows gave chase,
hounds sniffing for a trace,
only to be met with the tears of a summer rain.

j.e.dante

[Tanning Red]

Grass clippings take advantage of my nose;
sneezes accompany the rolling warmth in the air.
It's traipsing across my elongated face,
my pigment the ruler that measures
time spent in relief of artificial glow.
Energy efficiency shakes in well-worn wake,
but pales in contrast to the mother's warmth.
It's been a while since I've felt the light of day.
Unceremoniously, a dove introduces itself to a window,
leaving a dusty imprint on display
upon a window whose physicality sits transparently.
The pain is hard to place.
I continue to pace in the solar embrace,
weighing the cost of melanoma
to my comatose state.

[Watching Paint Dry]

It seems to me that things
around here never change,
and I'm the only one who can see it.
The trouble is my feet are propped,
and my ass is always seated.

j.e.dante

[Exhausted Fumes]

We crave the vast expanses of space,
the last of the greatest frontiers,
on the backs of fiery steeds raised,
extending our dwindling years.
Fortunes are made in wages and graves;
fossil fuels always abundant.
Wealth climbs and reclines to heaven's gates,
regrettable dunces as pundits.
Maestros who've stroked the wide blue yonder,
rendered landscapes infallible.
None who're alive survey the skies—
requisites for their survival.
Countdowns commence, victory in grasp,
as roaring flame scorches the earth.
Legions force mounted for requiem;
void vacuum eclipses their worth.

[A Warning]

The foul dwelt here for so long,
and in this place, they will remain.
Broken and battered, they sit and wait
for what they cannot foresee.
The path was clouded long ago;
from first light, the dark must always follow.
This, the open letter of a man who's seen the past,
written to the world's children so that they might last:
"Wage wars without weapons, but with a steadfast
resolve, to heed what is written, and preserve these
sacred halls."

j.e.dante

[Ghoulish]

Will-o'-wisps connect dots
between bouts of sleep,
marauding ghoul walkers
and floating creeps,
static-ridden stalkers
sniffing for feet,
thwarted as always
by linens and sheets.

Lengthy Momentary Lapses on Purpose

[Island]

Are you truly empathetic?
Are you glad it wasn't you?
Such a modest aesthetic
through plight you accrue.

j.e.dante

[Faded]

Half-empty beer bottles sit, sweating in the hands of swaying twenty-one pluses, sharing in the shrill, uneven cascade of colorful noise flowing through twin amplifiers, whose sharp melodies slice cleanly through this perfect concoction of moisture and heat. Texas summer nights are nights that just cannot be beat.

[Twelve Phases]

In rhythm there is triumphant vigor,
irate to whims that so easily stray.
Lacey time bends curvature to figure;
caressing fingers glide as flush betrays.
Reconciled my chest forlorn, it heaves,
indentured to work, to sorrowful song.
Guised, I walk amidst the changing leaves;
seasons pass me by, so have I prolonged.
Wolves howl as I to your moonlit pigment,
darkest curls part, baring pointed breast's peak.
Cadence upon thy personage,
spirit eclipsed by tender lips, nectar so sweet.
Morning breaks; I awake, tangled in branch.
Mourning I await another moonlit dance.

j.e.dante

[Nineteen Ninety -Nine]

Summer dripped salt to sand; ice cream for dinner plans; shells rinsed by the sea. New Jersey shored up my innocence, sunblock burning my eyes, sunburn scorches where trunks slip. Throwing a fit for a blip, forgetting VHS tapes rewinding—introductions to the next thirteen years.
Castles conquered by the tide. The Moon abides our presence. The sand is bitter. Seagulls caw from flamboyant, rented bungalows. Bags packed separately this time. Navy van that's older than me, front seat belts that roll themselves. Miles pass as daylight fades. We park and pass-through automatic sliding doors, leading to stark, dimly lit corridors. Gold-handled, wheeled carriages brimming with exclusive cargo. I hitch a ride: Lobby, Elevator, Hotel Key, Empty room.
Embracing a crowd, bending a knee, crumbling squeeze, wet patter on my neck. A door closes, then I leave. Alone.

[Things Mothers Shouldn't See]

Six: such an innocent number.
Glue-stick collages and picture books.
Homeschool broadened horizons.
Penmanship of authors that can scarcely read.
Top-secret, button-clipped page turners.
Fugitives glaring up at a mattress.
Magazine clippings sprinkled about:
Designer hoes and booties in rose,
rows of scantily clad glee.
And there sits single-digit me,
innocently collecting those greatest finds,
inexplicably lacking any inkling of what it all means.

j.e.dante

[Ashtrays]

Ashtrays are like my room when I was seven—filthy until reprimanded, yet bottomlessly messy when addressed. The words I recall were never expressly to clean it. Goodnight was only withheld so long as there was no route around. So, leaping from bed, resounding caterwauls articulating, I'd wade through the debris, shifting this and that as I'd go, until good old Dad's humor twisted and elbowed to tuck me in for the night. You know, Ashtrays are more like me in my room when I was seven: a charred opportunist hounding for the boon in the quickest fixes, howling despite himself for goodnight kisses.

[Folly]

When you come across an old trunk that's stumped,
whose diction cannot be made to convey,
you are barking up the wrong tree, you stunt—
it's time to branch out to make more headway.
You'll gasp and grasp for homely impression,
heir to a world without err to filter,
queried motive in deliberation,
in your task, becoming quite bitter.
This, an homage to reckless abandon,
the artistry in a thought not thinking,
exercising one's self of a stand-in—
just don't forget to keep breathing.

j.e.dante

[Proliferation's Discretion]

The tomb shrouded the sunken silhouette's form, emancipating it from the cordial salutations of somber souls, uplifting it beyond the computations of valiant cartographers, nestling it amongst the vastitudes that surmount our outer limits, that which pesters the edges of our vision when night is looming.
Shadows falling across the land as silence draws nigh, precipitating tendrils, leaching the colors from all that surrounds, stealing the blissful dreamscape from those who commissioned its timeless nature tamed. Whether the life we shared always held an expiration, or the numbers ticked faster than we could count, I wish for nothing, my wildflower. You were truly enough.

Lengthy Momentary Lapses on Purpose

[Millisecond of Hell]

Waking up is hardest
when you'd rather just forget.
The past whispers
sweet nothings as we drift.
Stop these voices once they start!
Can't stop the voices in the dark.
No night, no day can take this away.
I'm plagued by the things they say.
The shadows lurk in my wake,
a marriage of fates.
They wait for me there,
a realization of all my fears.

j.e.dante

[Bolstering Your Breeches to Bursting]

Rioted applause purchased,
lumbering self-admiration.
A simple social cue is met:
I am epitomized radiance.
Bow to your inner zealot,
and compromise your ideals with me.
Look how your posture withers;
watch as your cultivated crop bakes,
parched before harvest,
crumbling the loaf that was never imagined.
But it is not your imagination that realizes me.
Awestruck, you will hang onto my every lasting word,
until at least you trundle toward a back door
and a ruby glow, giving last wind a renouncement,
because you will never surmount this peak.
And then I speak:
Expletive. Expletive.
Choice observation.
Unconscientious comment.
Crickets steal the show, as I am unceremoniously
chauffeured to the window.
Rendezvous with a four-paneled reality eminent.
Zion was never meant for men to circumvent,
lest they wish their tongues nailed to crosses
that bare no spiritual significance.

Lengthy Momentary Lapses on Purpose

[The Simple Things]

Oh, the life of a fly:
To wake in the morning,
eat shit,
and die.

j.e.dante

[String Theory]

When it's all said and done,
life would have been
some kind of tragic
if I let what I thought you'd say
get in the way of forever.

[Here We Go Again]

She draped herself across my chest,
whispered, "This is it."
And if you listened close enough,
you could just make out
the dingy old, hand-me-down Afghan
grumbling from the hall closet.

j.e.dante

[Poor Sport]

I was racking my brain
for an avant-garde way
to profess my infatuation,
some grandiose gesture,
a spectacular proposition
to trick you into falling for a stray.
But the not-so-subtle truth:
The point was made moot
when you made the first move
and laughed at my hopeless display.

[First World Problems]

Three generations is all it took
to leave us destitute, jobless, and broke.
Three tree branches to fan the blaze,
zealots consumed in their colloquial rage.
And for what? To not be your mother's daughter?
Not to follow in the footsteps
spelled out by your only father?
If respect is earned, not given,
then why the hell would we give in?
Begin to claim treason over reason,
because we believe in instant gratification
over seasons of self-preservation.
But shit, that's precisely where we sit,
on a pile of washed-up, worn-out,
fear-mongering hypocrites—
those who reside in the houses
of our ancestors and their wives,
who went to war and gave their lives,
so we could survive into our time.
While they thrive on tax evasion
and childish persuasion,
we squandered blessings over shitty pride,
picking fights with bipolar, bipartisan sides
that can't ever actually pick a side,
but damn are they good at drawing lines.
If lives depended on co-signs,
hear me out: We'd all be dead.

j.e.dante

[Mannequin]

I wish I could be the men you read about
late at night, when you think I'm asleep.
Evocative, sultry, dense, and dull—
 just a plot device to move your story forward.
Things would be simpler that way.

[Ellipsis]

If hello ever becomes goodbye,
don't weep for what once was.
You won't need mental gymnastics
and apologetics, social proofs,
or proper documentation
to prove we had a good thing going:
The memories will last you a lifetime.

j.e.dante

[Black hole]

As we drift through the nether,
my heart aches as I contemplate
the expanses of forever—
or whatever.

Lengthy Momentary Lapses on Purpose

[Thoughts of You]

I wish I could hack a road to nowhere,
picket a fence, seed a lawn,
and let the seasons wash over me.
Maybe then, in that fortress of quiet solitude,
the creek of the trees, the breath of the breeze,
and the gurgle of the rippling brook
would coax you from the depths of my memory,
and one last whisper of "I love you"
would grace your lips, finally setting me free.
We could hitch a ride on the winds of time
for the rest of eternity,
grasping at forever, clasping each other close
until the mere concept of time forgets itself.

Thank you for taking this journey with me. If you were moved by these words, I would be deeply grateful if you shared your experience by leaving an honest review on Amazon. Your feedback is invaluable, and it helps my poetry find the readers it was meant for.

[About the Author]

J.e.dante is a poet whose work explores the intricate landscapes of the human mind, grappling with modern anxiety, existential ponderings, and the search for meaning. His verse is known for its raw honesty, sharp observation, and unique blend of cynicism and vulnerability. When not writing, he trades the solitude of verse for the chaos and comfort of family life. "Lengthy Momentary Lapses on Purpose" is his debut collection. Connect with j.e.dante and explore more of his work on Instagram.

J.E.DANTE

Coming Soon:

Perfecting Mediocrity in the Days of the Devil
A poetry collection

How much effort does it take to be just enough when the world is going to hell?

A new poetry collection by j.e.dante, author of *Lengthy Momentary Lapses on Purpose* dedicated to the sublime comfort of the low bar and the desperate art of the half-hearted success.

Look for Perfecting Mediocrity in the Days of the Devil—where true brilliance is strictly prohibited.

The Devils in the details...

www.ingramcontent.com/pod-product-compliance
Lightning Source LLC
Chambersburg PA
CBHW020935090426
42736CB00010B/1149